Wandering Woman: South Dakota

The Ultimate Road Trip: One Woman's Journey Across the United States by RV

Julie Bettendorf

Contents

Introduction

"Not all who wander are lost." JRR Tolkien

Are you sure? I thought to myself, as I tried not to panic. I was a long way from anything familiar, but that was how it should be. I had driven thousands of miles on dusty, pothole-filled roads. It's often on the worst roads that you can discover something truly amazing.

My dusty CRV was parked beside me, containing one restless dog and a variety of snack bags, all empty by now. There were no buildings in sight, no cars or people or movement at all. Only the constant humming of the insects as they buzzed around my head.

I turned to my left – another straight road that trailed off into the distance. I glanced over to the right, then behind me – two more barely discernible roads stretched out into the abyss. I was in a four-way intersection with no signs, no sense of direction, and no sign of life for several miles. No cell service either. *Damn*, I thought. *I'm lost.*

How did I get here? I couldn't help but feel like this little intersection was a cruel metaphor for life. I began to daydream, imagining each road might transport me back to a different time, a different role in my life, and a different me.

If I took the road from whence I came, it could lead me all the way back to Oregon, back to my cheating third husband, back to a life of loneliness and solitude. There is no greater loneliness than being married to someone who isn't actually present in your life.

If I took the road to my left, perhaps it could take me back to my career as a dental hygienist, a job I hated deep down in my soul. There is something so disengaging about cleaning teeth for a living. It's a disgusting, smelly way to get a paycheck. It pays well, which is great, but the best part is the huge gob of friends I enjoy to this day.

Or maybe the road to my right, *yes – maybe that's the path*, I imagined. Maybe it could take me back to my real treasure, my kids. Back to their smiling, innocent faces as toddlers, as they danced around the Christmas tree and their father and I were still married. Back when they still needed me for every little thing.

But, that was just it. I didn't feel needed anymore. My kids weren't toddlers anymore – they were both full-grown adults, and far too busy for me. My dental buddies were still working, but I wasn't. Dental hygiene had robbed me of the cartilage in my fingers, giving me severe, disabling arthritis. And, I wouldn't be returning to any more husbands either, because three marriages were quite enough for me.

All three of these paths, all three of these roles – the wife, the mother, and the dental hygienist – had seemingly been stripped from me within a year. I was lost and looking to find myself again.

The funny thing about this phrase, "not all who wander are lost" – is that, in my experience, wandering and being lost walk hand-in-hand with one another, and the expression can be flipped. In my experience, not all who are lost are wandering, and that is a real disservice to the beauty and clarity that the world has to offer.

When one becomes lost, wandering is the only option to guide oneself back to a path. After all, one could not come upon any dirt path at all without wandering.

I began wandering at an early age, both with my mind and with my feet. At eight years old, I was reading a book about archaeology and dreaming of one day seeing Egypt. I didn't follow a traditional path in high school either, going heavily into foreign languages, in hopes of one day using them.

At twenty-five years old, I divorced my first husband (the dental student who talked me into becoming a dental hygienist so I could work for him) and decided to give traveling a real shot. I took off for the Andes and Macchu Picchu, climbing up ancient Inca stone steps to reach the magnificent ruins.

Anyone who has been to Macchu Picchu will tell you there is something ethereal and deeply spiritual about the place. The ruins stretch out across the emerald green mountains, way up in the middle of the sky. Macchu Picchu gave me my first experience of feeling history. This trip inspired me to come back and complete a degree in archaeology, and I've been wandering ever since.

More travel followed including a backpack trip around Europe for three months, by myself, and trips to Britain, Italy, and Greece. I visited the burial places of Crusaders, mummies, and ancient kings. I happened upon the castle of my namesake in Bettendorf, Luxembourg, and wandered my way through European history.

My favorite excursion by far was finally seeing Egypt with my daughter in 2012. Just like my childhood dream envisioned, I rode a camel beneath the pyramids of Giza, with my head wrapped in some man's sweaty turban. It was perfect.

Traveling has always been my own personal antidote to pain. I went to Mexico after my first and second divorces, Canada after my third, and Italy after my dad died. Call it avoidance if you want, but I call it an accelerated form of healing in the purest sense of the word. I believe travel can heal your soul.

Wandering has always worked its wonders on me – made me feel renewed, rejoiceful, grateful, and purposeful. It's been my medicine.

So, as I stood in that intersection, I once again wondered how wandering had led me so astray this time. *What the hell am I supposed to do now?* It was then that I realized that one last path had not been considered yet – the path which stretched straight out in front of me. *Which role does this represent?* I pondered.

The answer smacked me in the face.

That last dirt road – the only path that could take me where I wanted to go, the only path that ever truly healed me or showed me the way – was the path of the traveler. The wife, the mother, and the hygienist roles – though valued in their time – were sitting in the bleachers now. It was time to welcome and enable my boldest, bravest, and perhaps most pivotal role yet:

The role of the Wandering Woman.

Why You Need to Take a Road Trip

A merica, the beautiful? I sure think so, but I didn't realize just how beautiful our country is until I embarked on traveling across the United States, full time, in a small RV.

The United States offers something for everyone. From spectacular beaches, austere mountains, to rolling plains, our country has it all. It's difficult to comprehend just how large and impressive our scenery is, until you experience it first-hand, with the ultimate road trip.

I also realized just how much of our history is missing from U.S. history I was taught as a kid. The history of our country didn't begin with the pilgrims landing on Plymouth Rock in the 1600s. Our history is far more ancient, with rock art and archaeological sites dating back over 12,000 years.

We owe a tremendous debt to early pioneers who tamed our land. The Mormons and other groups ventured into the great unknown with their families and their worldly possessions. Some of them pulled cumbersome handcarts across the country to settle in inhospitable, dangerous locations.

The goal of **Wandering Woman** is to bring history back to life and make it interesting again. I am presenting some famous sites, and many little-known ones. You will take the road-less-traveled with me, while we explore ghost towns, rock art sites, archaeological sites, and museums, to discover the colorful tapestry that is our country.

I present some history, including dates, but my goal is to present more of the real-life stories of history, including ghost stories, profiles in history, voices from the past, and moments in time, to give you, the reader, a deeper understanding of the context of history.

This is by no means an exhaustive list of places to visit. In fact, I encourage you to discover America for yourself, as I am doing, by making a trek across the land by car or RV. You can venture forth as the early explorers did, just a little more comfortably, with a lot less hardship.

I hope you enjoy this book and take a little time out to discover our beautiful country, and maybe even discover yourself in the process.

Safe Travels,

Julie Bettendorf

Welcome to Wandering Woman

This book is for you – the grieving empty nester mom, the be-grudged housewife, the woman in need of a drastic change in her life. Really, this book is for anyone with a passion for traveling. If you feel lost with no sense of direction or purpose in life, that's a bonus – this book will be even more appealing to you. And lastly, if you're a man reading this book, congratulations for holding a book with the word woman in the title. You're contributing to gender equality, and that's pretty neat.

I decided to combine three of my dearest loves – travel, history, and archaeology – and put them into a book because I believe wandering has the power to change your life. I have been to many areas of the world and have enjoyed too many outstanding experiences to list. However, by the time both my children moved out in 2017, I realized I was a stranger in my own country. It was the perfect time to explore a new country (my own) and discover a new me at the same time. I have been traveling for five years now, and I've upgraded to a small RV. I also have a new traveling companion, another sweet Sheltie, named Rosie. ***Wandering Woman*** is the chronicle of my journey across the United States, discovering the joy of getting lost and finding myself along the way.

Welcome to South Dakota

The Mount Rushmore State

South Dakota is a land sacred to Native Americans. When you spend time there, you can see why. Places like Bear Butte call to us, and remind us of the power and beauty of nature. South Dakotans are justly proud of their state and are some of the friendliest people you will ever meet. When you travel to South Dakota, you may want to stay awhile and enjoy the vast, rolling plains and small town atmosphere.

Five things to love about South Dakota:

- The spectacular scenery of Spearfish Canyon

- Historic Old West towns like Deadwood

- Old military forts like Fort Meade

- Famous memorial sculptures like Mount Rushmore

- Ancient fossil sites like the Mammoth Site

Dreams of South Dakota

"I learned more about the economy from one South Dakota dust storm that I did in all my years of college." **Hubert H. Humphrey**

"Babies are born bow-legged in South Dakota. By the age of 12, they can purchase guns. At 14, they can take their driving test. Fortunately, since the geographical area of South Dakota can accommodate both France and Germany, but has a population of only 750,000, the chances of hitting anything are pretty slim." **Clive Sinclair**

"My mother and father, with my newborn brother and me in the backseat of the 1938 Ford sedan that would be our family car for the next decade, moved to that hastily constructed Army ammunition depot called Igloo, on the alkaline and sagebrush landscape of far southwestern South Dakota. I was three years old." **Tom Brokaw**

Famous South Dakota Citizens

- Cheryl Ladd 1951-current, actress

- Eddie Little Sky 1926-1997, actor

- Laura Ingalls Wilder 1867-1957, author

- Red Cloud 1822-1909, Oglala Lakota Chief

- Sitting Bull 1831-1890, Hunkpapa Lakota Chief

- Bob Barker 1923-2023, television game show host

- Tom Brokaw 1940-current, television journalist

Early South Dakota

Historic D.C. Booth Fish Hatchery

Early Deadwood

Early South Dakota Justice

Slim Buttes

***S*lim Buttes Battle Site** in South Dakota shows off some spectacular scenery. It's also very historic. On September 9th and 10th of 1876, still reeling from defeat at the Battle of the Little

Bighorn the previous June, General Crook began to systematically hunt Sioux Indians. He sent Captain Anson Mills to Deadwood for supplies.

Mills found a village of 37 lodges, camped on the eastern slope of Slim Buttes, and attacked. Chief American Horse was fatally wounded and four warriors were dead. The band of Sioux surrendered.

Two soldiers and a civilian scout were killed. They are memorialized at a site on Slim Buttes.

How to get to Slim Buttes:

The Slim Buttes Battle Site is located off South Dakota Highway 20, about a quarter mile west of Highway 79, and roughly one mile west of the town of Reva.

My story:

I was tired when I got to Slim Buttes Campground. I had been driving for hours, and it was hot, and I was sweaty. All these facts are poor excuses for what was about to happen. The campground was lovely, remote, and deserted. The campsites were also elevated, with steep drop-offs on both sides. Me and my flip-flops decided to back into a spot. Unfortunately, my sweat, flip-flops, and tired driving skills were no match for the campground, and I rolled my RV. My first thought was to get out, so I dragged my terrified dog, Rosie, and hoisted her out of the RV and onto the ground above. Then, I pulled myself out. I sat for awhile, pondering my life choices.

I decided I needed help, so I began to walk, and found the one lone guy living at the campground. Thoughts of "House of Wax," and every other horror movie flashed through my head, but I called out anyway. A young man in a cowboy hat stepped out. After I told him about my idiotic accident, he stroked his chin and calmly said, "Well, let's take a look."

On our way to the RV, I asked him what he was doing up there, and he said, "I'm a taxidermist." More thoughts of horror movies flashed in my head and how he was going to murder Rosie and I and stuff us for later use. When we got to the RV, he stroked his chin again and calmly said,"I'm gonna need some help. I'll be back in about 30 minutes."

True to his word, in about 30 minutes I could see his truck coming back, followed by two more trucks. He and his buddies jumped out, surveyed the scene of the crime, and got to work. Thanks to several thick tow ropes, the power of the pickup truck, and these guys goodness and kindness, they had me out in under an hour. I was beside myself with joy and asked them if I could give them some money or buy them some beer, and they looked at me, puzzled, and said, "Ma'am that's what we do here in South Dakota. We help people."

I tell this story often, and think how lucky I was to be in South Dakota.

Spearfish

Spearfish is a wonderful town, with a spectacular city park and campground right in the middle of it. If that's not enough, a beautiful creek runs down through the middle of town.

The city park has a historic stone building built in 1880 which used to be a meat house owned by Rudolf Kroll of Lead.

Spearfish was founded in 1876 by a group of pioneers from Iowa. The Burlington Railroad came through town in 1893, running from Spearfish to Deadwood, through the length of spectacular Spearfish Canyon.

As you walk around town, look out for the D.C. Booth Historic National Fish Hatchery. It's one of the oldest fish hatcheries in the west, begun in 1899. The D.C. Booth Fish Hatchery was instrumental in bringing trout to the Black Hills area.

There is a historic building on site, and an underwater viewing area to watch the beautiful trout.

Spearfish is full of beauty. In fact, it's so beautiful, a scene from the movie Dances with Wolves was filmed in Spearfish Canyon.

How to get to Spearfish:

Spearfish is located 10 miles east of the Wyoming border, off US I-90.

Deadwood

G eorge Custer came into South Dakota's Black Hills in 1874, with orders to map the area. He had 1000 men with him, some of whom were geologists. These geologists located gold in the Black Hills, and soon, prospectors flooded into the new camp called *Deadwood.* The town was named for the many burned trees in the area.

By 1876, there were an estimated 10,000 gold seekers in Deadwood and the surrounding area. There were also 166 businesses in Deadwood, selling useful goods and services.

Butter and eggs were highly sought after, with one store selling 18 tons of butter in 3 months. Retailers known as the Gardner Brothers brought in several thousand eggs, wrapped individually and packed in barrels full of oats.

Deadwood is still a bustling, busy place, with tourism and gaming replacing gold mining. You can visit many historic buildings and interesting areas.

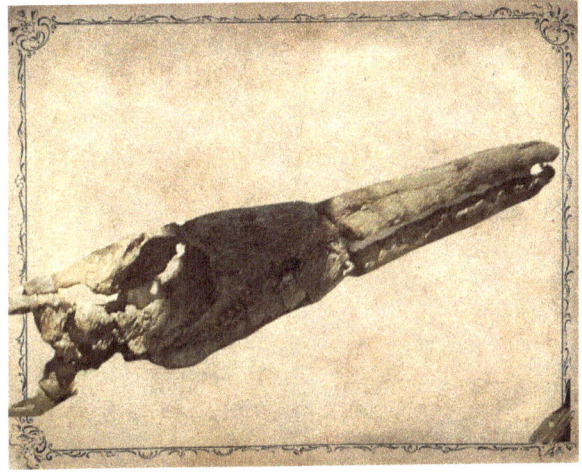

Deadwood also has some fascinating museums, including the Adams Museum, containing early mining days and Wild Bill Hickok artifacts. The museum also has a plesiosaur skeleton discovered in the Black Hills in 1934.

One of my favorite pieces in the museum is a table and chair set containing 4500 sections of intricately inlaid wood.

Don't miss the spot where Wild Bill Hickok was shot in the back of the head by Jack McCall on August 2, 1876, as he played cards. When Hickok died, he allegedly was holding a hand of black aces and black 8s, known as the "Dead Man's Hand."

How to get to Deadwood:

Deadwood is located about 13 miles southwest of Sturgis, on Hwy. 14A.

A word about causes of death in Deadwood:

In Mt. Moriah cemetery, there are several colorful and unusual causes of death listed on tombstones, including being hanged by vigilantes, drinking bad whiskey, eating 14 hard-boiled eggs, being struck with a bar glass, and God-knows.

Ghost story:

Marshall Seth Bullock's ghostly form has been sighted walking the halls of the Bullock Hotel in Deadwood. The most famous story is that of a young child who got locked out of his bedroom. He was helped back to his room by a kindly older man. The next day, the boy identified the man who helped him, from a picture on the wall. The picture was of Seth Bullock. Items in Seth's Cellar Restaurant have been seen moving on their own. No less than five people witnessed a glass come flying off a shelf and crashing to the floor. Still others have witnessed a "cowboy" roaming the halls and smoking a cigar. Lewis, Fisk, Shadley, Wennes

Profiles in history:

Pioneer preacher Henry Weston Smith was born January 10, 1827 in Ellington, CT. He first came into the Black Hills to the town of Custer in 1876. He followed the gold seekers into Deadwood. Preacher Smith was known to work 6 days a week, and then walk 20 miles to preach 2 sermons on Sundays. Preacher Smith was shot and killed on his way to preach in Crook City. A monument stands near the spot where Preacher Smith died.

James Butler Hickok, famously known as "Wild Bill" Hickok was born on May 27, 1837, in Homer, Illinois. He was over six feet tall, and fast with a gun. Hickok served as a peace officer in Kansas. He then headed to Missouri, where he joined up as a sharpshooter for the Union army during the Civil War. In 1872, he joined Buffalo Bill's Wild West Show, often portraying Custer.

When gold was found in the Black Hills of South Dakota, Wild Bill Hickok went to Deadwood. It was here in Deadwood that Wild Bill was shot to death while playing poker in the No. 10 Saloon on August 2, 1876. Wild Bill is buried in Mount Moriah Cemetery in Deadwood.

Martha Jane Canary-Burke, famously known as "Calamity Jane" was born in Princeton, Missouri in 1852. Her parents died when she was 13, leaving her in charge of caring for herself and five siblings. She moved the family to Fort Bridger, Wyoming, where she worked as a prostitute and laundress to feed her family members.

Calamity Jane was many things including a railroad worker, stage-coach driver, nurse, and scout for General Custer. Jane arrived in Deadwood together with Wild Bill Hickok in 1876. Calamity Jane was devoted to Wild Bill. When Calamity Jane died in 1902, she was buried next to him in Mount Moriah Cemetery in Deadwood.

Fort Meade

*F**ort Meade*** was founded in 1878, and named for General George C. Meade. It was the home of Custer's 7th Cavalry. Today, it's a medical facility of the Veteran's Administration.

Fort Meade was also where the "Star Spangled Banner" was first played on the parade ground in 1892. It became the national anthem in 1931 by an act of congress.

The fort contains a fascinating museum, with a diverse collection of artifacts, including pieces created by some of General Rommel's German troops who were held there during World War II. This ship-in-a-bottle art piece was created in the 1940s by a German POW.

One of my favorite pieces is the safe used by the 7th cavalry from 1878 to 1888. Kevin Costner used it for the Fort Hayes scene in the movie Dances with Wolves.

Another favorite piece is a petroglyph stone found on the banks of nearby Bear Butte Creek.

The museum at Fort Meade also has historical photographs, including this one of Comanche, the only horse in the Army to survive the Battle of Little Bighorn. Comanche was owned by Captain Myles Keogh, who died in the battle.

How to get to Fort Meade:

Fort Meade is located a few miles east of Sturgis, South Dakota.

Profiles in history:

Alice Ivers Duffield Tubbs Huckert, also known as **Poker Alice,** was born February 17, 1851 in Devon, England. When she was 12, Alice and her parents emigrated to Virginia. She later moved to Leadville, Colorado, and met her first husband, Frank Duffield, who introduced her to poker. Frank was killed in a mining accident, so Alice became a Faro dealer to support herself. She dealt faro in some famous towns, including Deadwood. She met and married two more husbands, who both died. Alice began her life as a poker player, opening a gambling establishment in Sturgis, to entertain the soldiers at Fort Meade. Alice became known as

Poker Alice, because she had a real poker face, not giving up any information about the hand she held. Poker Alice died on February 27, 1930 at the age of 79.

A moment in time:

On the night of November 10, 1879, Major Marcus Reno, famous for surviving the Battle of the Little Bighorn, peeped through the window of Ella Sturgis' home, to gaze at the beautiful lady. Ella Sturgis happened to be the daughter of General Sturgis, the commander at Fort Meade. Ella saw Reno looking in at her, and told her father. General Sturgis had Reno stand trial, and Reno was thrown out of the Army. Reno died in poverty iin 1967. After his death, Reno was exonerated, and his remains were moved to join his comrades in the cemetery at the Battle of Little Bighorn.

Bear Country
U.S.A.

*B**ear Country U.S.A.* is an outstanding drive-through wildlife park. The stars are the black and brown bears which wander in and out among the cars, but there is much more to see.

You will see sections containing pronghorn antelope, deer, reindeer, mountain lions, arctic wolves, bighorn sheep, and elk, all in huge, beautiful enclosures.

After you have driven through the park, there is a wildlife walkway for small animals, including badgers and porcupine.

Don't miss the amazingly cute bear cubs. Bear Country U.S.A. is a wonderful way to spend a few hours.

How to get to Bear Country U.S.A:

Bear Country U.S.A. is located 8 miles south of Rapid City on Hwy. 16.

Four Mile Old West Town

*F**our Mile Old West Town*** was originally known as Moss City, named after the Moss family, early pioneers to the area. The name was changed to Four Mile when a stagecoach stop was built.

Today, Four Mile Old West Town is a museum, with a delightful conglomeration of old buildings, complete with authentic furnishings.

Check out one of the largest buildings, the hotel. This hotel had a bedroom which rented out for travelers, and a boarding house room for women who worked for the hotel, and a salesmen room for traveling salesmen.

One of the more picturesque buildings is the red fur trappers shed. It has a lived-in look, with furs hanging from the walls.

Beaver was a popular fur because it could shed water. It was important to keep warm and dry, because pneumonia was common, and often fatal.

The saloon was the gathering place for many early mining towns.
Many saloons also sold supplies and were known as roadhouses.

Another fascinating building is the Undertaker's office, complete with an old wooden embalming table.

Back in the day, it was common to make the body fit the coffin, not the other way around.

No wild west town is complete without the jail. The jail in Four Mile was moved from Ward, South Dakota.

There is lots of history to be found here, including very informative printed material at each of the buildings. I have no favorites at Four Mile, because each building is equally wonderful.

Take your time and enjoy the various coaches and wagons on the property too.

How to get to Four Mile Old West Town:

Four Mile Old West Town is located in Custer, South Dakota, off Hwy. 16.

A word about mileage in the Old West:

The names which include the word "mile" actually have meaning. "Four Mile" indicated the presence of a stagecoach stop and watering hole, "Nine Mile" indicated the presence of a horse barn, "Twelve Mile" indicated you could find a meal and lodging, and "Eighteen Mile" meant the presence of another watering hole.

Mystic &
Rochford

M*ystic* is a beautiful little ghost town near Spearfish Canyon. It was founded in 1876 as a mining town, originally named Sitting Bull. The town gained importance when the railroad came through town.

Mystic's main business was the George Frink sawmill, which operated from 1919 to 1952. After the sawmill closed, Mystic became a ghost town. Parker, Lambert

The tiny town of **Rochford** was founded by two men named Hughes and Rochford in 1877. One year later it had a population of over 500 people. It's famous for the Moonshine Gulch Saloon which opened in 1910, during the gold rush in the Black Hills.

How to get to Mystic & Rochford:

Mystic is located off County Road 231, about 20 miles west of Rapid City and 12 miles north of Hill City.

Rochford is located on Hwy 85, off the Rochford exit.

Ghost story:

The Moonshine Gulch Saloon is reportedly haunted by the ghost of the former owner. It is believed that the owner is buried underneath the building. In fact, the current owners found a tombstone believed to be hers. The tombstone now lies underneath part of the building. Paranormal happenings include objects dropping for no apparent reason, lights not working, and the feeling of someone brushing by visitors. Ghosts of miners have also been seen and noises of mining have been heard coming from the woods. Lewis, Fisk

Keystone

T he ***Keystone Townsite*** was laid out in 1891 by founders
William Franklin, Thomas Blair, and Jacob Reed. The name

Keystone came from the Masonic symbol and one of the town's mines. It's a quaint little town which began as a gold mining camp.

Towering above Keystone are the remnants of the Big Thunder Gold Mine, established in 1892, and the Holy Terror Mine, named for Jennie Franklin, William Franklin's wife.

As you walk around town, you can see Halleys Store, built in 1895.
It's the oldest continuously running business in Keystone.

The inside of Halleys Store is a menagerie of goods of all kinds. Some are artifacts, and some are for sale.

Don't miss the log schoolhouse, from the 1890s. Miss Mary Whee-
lock taught 40 students there in 1894 through 1895.

Nearby is the Keystone school, built in 1899. The building cost $10,000 and housed 300 students.

How to get to Keystone:

Keystone is located off Hwy. 40, about 2 miles northeast of Mount Rushmore.

Ghost story:

There is a legend about ***Tommyknockers*** that are said to haunt many mining camps. Tommyknockers got their name from Cornish miners who believed that little men lived underground and caused the knocking with their tiny hammers. Some early miners believed Tommyknockers were good spirits who were warning of an impending mine collapse. Others believed that the person who heard the knocking would die. Still others believed that Tommyknockers were the spirits of miners who had died during a cave-in. Some miners even left offerings of food and drink to appease the Tommyknockers.

Mount Rushmore

T he name ***Mount Rushmore,*** was coined in the 1880s by a
teamster who had a passenger named Charles Rushmore.
The man asked the teamster for the name of the mountain, and

since it didn't have a name as yet, the teamster and Rushmore named it after the New York lawyer. Rushmore would later donate $5,000 to the monument and the monumental undertaking.

Mount Rushmore carving began in 1927, by master sculptor Gutzon Borglum. From 1927 through 1941, over 360 people worked to complete the monument. If the carvings were complete figures, they would be about 465 feet tall. Just the faces themselves are 60 feet tall.

Lincoln has a sparkle to his eye, which is actually a block of granite 12 inches long.

Borglum died in 1941, with the sculpture still incomplete. His son, Lincoln, completed the monument.

How to get to Mount Rushmore:

Mount Rushmore is located near Keystone, South Dakota, off Hwy. 244.

Voices from the past:

"The union of these four presidents carved on the face of the everlasting Black Hills of South Dakota...will be distinctly American in its conception, in its magnitude, in its meaning." **President Calvin Coolidge, August 10, 1927.**

Custer State Park

C uster State Park is heaven on earth. The park is spectacularly beautiful, and packed with wildlife, including a large
herd of bison, bighorn sheep, pronghorn antelope, and prairie

dogs. You may see them all by driving the 18 mile Wildlife Loop Road.

The park is named for General Custer, who entered the Black Hills in 1874. The story was he was going to map out the area and find a site for a new military post, but the reality was, he was looking for gold.

Custer's expedition did find gold in an area known as French Creek, and thus began the Black Hills gold rush of the 1870s.

There are several historic sites within Custer State Park, one of which is the Gordon Stockade. The original stockade was built in 1874, to protect a group of pioneers and settlers led by John Gordon.

The group included 26 men, one woman, one boy, six wagons, 15 yoke of oxen, six horses, and a donkey. The woman who came with the group was Annie Tallent, the first white woman to set foot in the Black Hills.

Another fantastically beautiful drive within the park is on Iron Mountain Road, which is another 18 miles. It's packed with spectacular bends and curves, with each view more breathtaking than the last. Iron Mountain Road travels through several rustic tunnels blasted into the rock, and you can take this road up to Mount Rushmore.

How to get to Custer State Park:

The Custer State Park Visitor's Center in located at the intersection of US Hwy. 16A and Wildlife Loop Road.

Voices from the past:

"Some of the members of the first expedition returned to the hills during the summer of 1875, others in the spring of 1876-while a few never returned." **Annie Tallent, 1878**

Crazy Horse Memorial

T he *Crazy Horse Memorial* is the world's largest carving on a mountain that is still unfinished. In 1939, Lakota Chief Standing Bear commissioned Korczak Ziolkowski to create a memorial to a Native American hero, Crazy Horse.

The first blast in what would later become the face of Crazy Horse began on June 3, 1948. The earliest work on the sculpture was done by Ziolkowski and his family, including his wife and their ten children.

Ziolkowski passed away in 1982, so additional work was completed by his wife and children. They completed the face of Crazy Horse in 1998.

Now, you can see the face of Crazy Horse, but in time, you will see him riding his horse and pointing to the Black Hills, indicating his famous line "My lands are where my dead lie buried." The entire sculpture will be 563 feet high and 641 feet wide. The face alone measures 87 feet high.

In addition to the magnificent sculpture, the Indian Museum of North America is at the site. It's actually five museums, and provides an outstanding overview of Native American history, art, and culture.

There are some fabulous pieces in the museum, including Crazy Horse's knife and sheath, and his pictographic signature. [Lewis, Fisk]

How to get to the Crazy Horse Memorial:

The Crazy Horse Memorial is located between the towns of Hill City and Custer off Hwy. 16/385.

Profiles in History:

Crazy Horse was a Lakota Sioux warrior born in the 1840s near what is now Rapid City, South Dakota. He was known to be a brilliant tactician and fierce fighter and leader. Conflict began when prospectors and settlers came into the Black Hills, seeking gold. They crossed into reservation lands, violating the treaty the U.S. government had with the Lakota.

General Crook was tasked with managing the situation. Crazy Horse joined with the Cheyenne, waging war on Crook's troops, forcing their withdrawal. Crazy Horse then joined Sitting Bull to wage war at the Battle of the Little Bighorn in Montana. Crazy

Horse and his tribe suffered from starvation and cold, so Crazy Horse surrendered to General Crook at the Red Cloud Agency in Nebraska on May 6, 1877. He was confined at Fort Robinson, and died there on September 5, 1877. He was just 35 years old.

Fun Facts about the Crazy Horse Memorial:

- Crazy Horse's face measures 87'6" high and 58'1" wide

- From the forehead to the bridge of the nose measures 32 feet

- Crazy Horse has a nose that is 27'6 long, and protrudes out 8'8"

- The eye openings & eyelids are 17'9" and 8'8" high

- The pupils have a diameter of 1'9"

- The head of Crazy Horse's horse measures 219' high

- The ears are 45' long

- The eyes are 16' wide and 13' high

- The nostrils have a diameter of 25' and a 9' depth

Hot Springs

Hot Springs has some outstanding things to see, including the town itself. Many of the buildings are made of native sandstone blocks and date from the 1890s.

The town is lovely, with a warm creek running down through the middle of it, and a wonderful meandering path you can take that leads you by some of the historic buildings, including the stately Evans Hotel.

There is an eclectic pioneer museum that sits dramatically above the town. It's housed in the 1893 schoolhouse.

There are over 15 rooms housing everything from old tools to old medical and dental equipment, to pioneer toys, and everything in between.

One of my favorite artifacts is this wonderful children's farm animal set made of tin.

As you walk around the town of Hot Springs, don't miss the Historic Wood Jail, which was found within the walls of a house in town during demolition.

The jail, built in 1885, is the oldest wooden jail in South Dakota. Calamity Jane may have spent the night in this jail in 1895.

How to get to Hot Springs:

Hot Springs is about 58 miles southwest of Rapid City, off Hwy. 18.

A moment in time:

On January 12, 1888, one of the worst blizzards ever recorded sped across the Great Plains states, producing a wall of ice that froze everything in its path. The 1888 blizzard became known as "The Schoolchildren's Blizzard," because many of the victims were schoolchildren. The blizzard blew out of Canada and landed down upon North Dakota in the early morning, South Dakota during the morning recess for school children, and Nebraska when school was soon to be dismissed.

When the blizzard had passed, dead animals and people were found frozen to death across the prairie. There were children on their way home from school, found frozen in large drifts of snow, frozen standing up against a tree, or frozen in a haystack. It is estimated that between 250 and 500 people died in the blizzard of 1888.

The Mammoth Site

T he ***Mammoth Site*** is a major attraction in Hot Springs, South Dakota. About 26,000 years ago, a large pond was here, providing a steady supply of water and grass for the mammoths.

The mammoths went in, but could not get back out, because of slippery, wet shale surrounding the pond. As a result, at least 61 mammoths are being unearthed from this ancient pond site at the time of this writing.

The Mammoth Site contains both Woolly and the larger, Columbian mammoths, along with camels and short-faced bear. The Mammoth Site is now the largest collection of in-situ mammoth remains in the world. All of the mammoth hip bones in the sinkhole are male, so these were adolescent males forced out of the herd.

The site was discovered in 1974 when bulldozing began for a new housing development. In the fall of 1975 a skull was unearthed. In 1976, a decision was made to leave the bones as they are. The site became the Mammoth Site. A beautiful circular structure has been built above the sinkhole, so you can view the excavations in 360 degrees. It's truly amazing.

Only 25 feet of the deposit has been excavated, and there are least 67 feet of deposits at the Mammoth Site.

How to get to the Mammoth Site:

The Mammoth Site is located at 1800 US 18 Bypass, Hot Springs, SD.

Badlands

You shouldn't go through South Dakota without visiting the ***Badlands***. The Badlands are what many people envision when they think of South Dakota. The Badlands got its name because in the 1800s, it was known as a "bad land to cross."

The Badlands are immense, spread out over 244,000 acres. They contain a wealth of fossils which are 23 to 25 million years old, including ancient marine reptiles, because the Badlands were once a sea.

Other fossils excavated in the badlands include camels, crocodiles, saber-tooth cats, three toed horses, rhinoceroses, and dinosaurs. Humans have lived in the area for the last 11,000 years. During the 1890s, Native Americans gathered in the Badlands for ghost dances. The Badlands was established as a National Monument in 1939.

Before you get to the Badlands, stop by the ghost town of *Scenic*, named for its scenic location. There is not much left of the town except for a few run-down buildings, but the desolation of it has a certain charm.

Scenic was a convenient stopping off point before entering the Black Hills. There was once a post office, the Longhorn Saloon, and a railroad depot. Today, the town of Scenic is owned by the Iglesia ni Cristo Church, based in the Philipines.

How to get to the Badlands & Scenic:

The Badlands are located about 60 miles east of Rapid City, off I-90.

The ghost town of Scenic is located at the western edge of the Badlands, off Hwy. 44.

A word about the Ghost Dance:

The Ghost Dance began among the Northern Paiute Native Americans of Nevada, in 1889. A Paiute leader named Wovoka had a prophecy that settlement by whites would stop, and the Native Americans could once again regain their homeland. The Ghost Dance was said to reunite the spirits of the dead with those of the living, to aid the Native Americans in the battle for their land and culture.

Fort Pierre

O n the site of ***Fort Pierre***, Joseph La Framboise built Fort
La Framboise in 1817, out of driftwood. It was a fur trading
outpost. In 1827, the American Fur Company bought out other fur

operations in the area and constructed Fort Pierre Chouteau in 1832, named after Pierre Chouteau, who ran the Western branch of the American Fur Company in St. Louis.

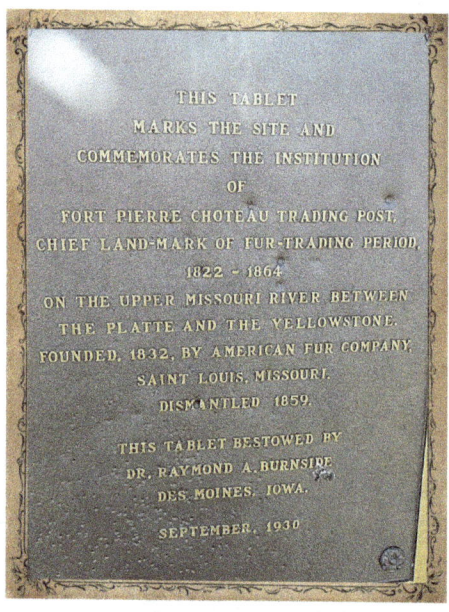

Fort Pierre Chouteau became the American Fur Company's main depot on the Upper Missouri River. It was sold to the Army in 1855, and abandoned in 1857. Today, all that is left of Fort Pierre is a memorial marker.

Fort Pierre is the site where the Verendyre Plate was buried in 1743, by two brothers, Louis-Joseph, and Francois Verendrye, to claim the area for France. The plate was found in 1913 by teenagers from Fort Pierre.

Fort Pierre has a very peaceful city park, right along the river. This spot has historic significance. It was here, on September 23-28, 1804, that Lewis and Clark met with the Teton Sioux. What began as a misunderstanding due to language differences became an armed conflict, which was diffused by the Sioux Chief Black Buffalo. The United States flag was first flown here in what would later become South Dakota.

How to get to Fort Pierre:

Fort Pierre is located in central South Dakota, off Hwy. 83.

A moment in time:

In 1913, Ethel Parrish, Hattie Foster, and George O'Reilly, were three teenagers from Fort Pierre out for a walk. Hattie saw an object sticking out of the ground. The three friends dug up a rectangular metal plate. Disinterested, they threw the plate back on the ground. George initially thought about selling the metal plate for scrap. When he went back into Fort Pierre, he met two town leaders and told them about the plate. The three went back and retrieved the plate, bringing it into Fort Pierre. The head of the South Dakota Historical Society, Doane Robinson, had researched and written extensively about the Verendyre brothers.

He knew immediately what the plate was, because it was described in the Verendyre brothers journal from 1743.

Voices from the past:

"I placed on an eminence near the fort (their camp) a tablet of lead, with the arms and inscription of the king and a pyramid of stones for Monsieur Le General; I said to the savages, who did not know of the tablet of lead I had placed in the earth, that I was placing these stones as a memorial of those who had come to their country."
Journal of the Verendyre Expedition, 1743.

Pierre

$\boldsymbol{P}$*ierre* is the capitol city of South Dakota and contains fine museums, including the South Dakota Cultural Heritage Center. The museum houses a wonderful collection of artifacts from the history of Native Americans of South Dakota up through South Dakota in the 21st century.

The Native American collections are striking, especially the Winter Count, a large piece of hide decorated with animals, warriors, and other designs, to signify the nights, moons, winters, and generations.

This Winter Count belonged to Sioux warrior Lone Dog, and is from the period 1800-1871.

Another stunning piece is this graceful horse effigy, carved to honor a horse killed in battle.

This skull rested on the top of the medicine pole used by Sitting Bull during the Ghost Dance at Standing Rock Reservation.

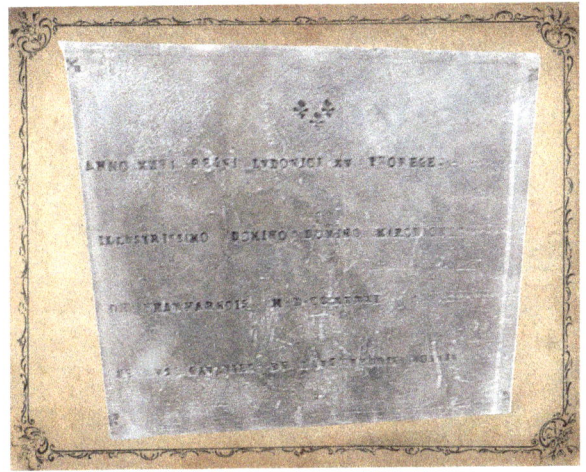

My favorite artifact within the museum is the Verendrye Plate, buried at Fort Pierre in 1743, by two brothers, Louis-Joseph, and Francois Verendrye, to claim the area for France. This double-sided plate translates as "In the 26th year of the reign of Louis XV, the most illustrious Lord, the Lord Marquis of Beauharnois, 1741, Pierre Gaultier De La Verendrye placed this." And on the back "Placed by the Chevalier Verendrye Louis La Londrette and A. Miotte, 30 March 1743." South Dakota State Historical Society

Pierre also has a wonderful little one-room schoolhouse from 1881, located in Steamboat Park. The schoolhouse began its life as a home for carpenters in the area. The citizens of Pierre repurposed the small building into a schoolhouse.

How to get to South Dakota Cultural Heritage Center:

The South Dakota Cultural Heritage Center is located at 900 Governors Drive, in Pierre.

A word about Code Talkers:

The Code Talkers were a vital group of Native Americans who sent coded messages in their native languages, to armies operating during World War I and World War II. 33 tribes of Native Americans participated, with 69 Native Americans being from South Dakota. The Germans were never able to decode the messages of the Code Talkers.

Fort Sisseton

F*ort Sisseton* was established in 1864 during the Civil War, to protect wagon trains against Indian attacks. It was named for the Sisseton Indian tribe who helped protect the fort.   The military were active at the fort from 1864 to 1889. The fort was built from local resources. The area around Fort Sisseton was opened to settlement in 1892.

The fort has many remaining stone structures, including the hospital, built in 1887, and the doctor's residence. In addition to treating patients, the doctor was also responsible for keeping track of animal sightings.

Today you can visit the north and south barracks, both built in 1864.

Don't miss the guardhouse jail, built in 1865. There were two rooms for guards with as many as 8 guards sleeping in one bed. The bed was tilted at the head to fight respiratory disease and tuberculosis.

Other buildings include the stables, built in 1865, the commanding officers quarters, built in 1882, and the magazine, built in 1867. The fort was closed in 1889.

Fort Sisseton also has a wonderful Visitor's Center, containing artifacts from the excavations at the Fort. Some of my favorite pieces include a Sioux drum from the 1860s, and bone dominoes.

How to get to Fort Sisseton:

Fort Sisseton is located near the town of Britton, in northeastern South Dakota.

Voices from the past:

"Very cold-very. My pony broke through the ice while I was watering him and he nearly perished with cold before I could get him back to the stable." **Soldier stationed at Fort Sisseton, Dec. 12, 1865.**

A word about military punishment:

At Fort Sisseton, there were 2 rooms for prisoners, who slept on the floor with no bedding. Punishments for prisoners included Woody the horse. When a man sat on it, his legs dangled. He was forced to lift a wooden sword with his right hand and keep it held straight out in front of him while holding the reins with his left hand. Prisoners had to sit like this for up to 8 hours. If the sword dropped, he had to start all over again.

Other punishments included wearing a barrel all day or carrying rock-filled feed sacks while still doing your duties.

Ghost story:

Fort Sisseton was built over the top of an Indian burial ground. In fact, when the flagpole was raised in 1864, the remains of an Indian grave were found. A soldier is said to haunt the barracks, with the sound of his boots echoing on the floor. The sound his feet make is said to come from a pair of Jefferson Brogan boots with wooden soles held in place by brass nails. These boots were worn by soldiers in the infantry in the 1800s. [Lewis, Fisk]

Favorite Places to Camp

*B**ear Butte State Park*** is my favorite campground in South Dakota. It is stunningly beautiful, and sacred to Native Americans. The campground has 15 non-electric campsites, with other non-electric campsites available. For reservations, visit https://gfp.sd.gov/parks/detail/bear-butte-state-park/

Spearfish City Campground is located in a beautiful spot, right in the middle of town. There are primitive campsites underneath the trees, and 55 electric campsites. There are showers at the campground, walking paths, and beautiful surroundings. For reservations, visit https://www.spearfish.gov/640/Reservation

Fort Sisseton Campground provides a great home base to discover Fort Sisseton and eastern South Dakota. The campground

has 14 electric sites and camper cabins. To make reservations, please visit https://reservations.gooutdoorssouthdakota.com/

Random Thoughts
What History Means to Me

F irst, let me start by sharing with you my opinion of what history isn't. History is not a collection of random dates, names, and places for you to memorize. History is not a dry and uninteresting class you have to pass to graduate.

I believe history is a tangible thing. You can actually *feel* history in the places you go, and the sights you see. I remember walking up to the Acropolis in Athens. I looked down at the well-worn marble steps and wondered about how many ancient philosophers had climbed these very steps, thousands of years ago.

You don't have to go far away to experience the *feeling* of history. If you are lucky enough to live in an old house, you may experience history in your own surroundings. You might say to yourself, *"If only these walls could talk."*

During my travels across the United States, I *felt* history in many, many places. If you travel across the country like I did, you will *feel* the wonderful history of our beautiful country for yourself, and you will never be the same. You will discover what it means to be an American.

Why I travel, and why you should too:

I decided to travel across the country by car because I wanted to rediscover America. When I first set out to explore the history of our country, I wanted to find out why America is the greatest country on earth, and what it means to be an American.

The politics of these United States can be frightening and polarizing. I prefer to focus on what unites us, not what divides us. What unites us is we all live in a spectacularly beautiful country, with warm, wonderful people.

I began my journey five years ago, starting out in my Honda CRV. I soon realized I loved the lifestyle, so now I travel in a small RV. From my small RV, I look out on a country with a unique and colorful, multicultural tapestry, unlike any other country on earth.

I have a degree in Archaeology, and a passion for all things archaeological. I love history, with a side love of paleontology. It is these three passions that I set my trip agenda around. I set out to discover the archaeological sites, history, and paleontological world of our country.

As I travel and write my books, I get asked all the time, especially by women, "What is it like to travel by yourself? Aren't you scared?" The truth is, I believe everyone should do what I did. It's a wonderful way to discover our country, and to rediscover yourself. The truth is, I'm scared not to travel. Traveling allows you to get to know yourself, in ways not possible when sitting on the couch watching TV.

We tend to spend a lot of our lives tuning out the world and our place within it. When you travel, you are quite literally forced to deal with your own thoughts, emotions, and feelings. You can discover yourself while traveling. You can come to understand what makes you who you are, and how you can perhaps become a better person. Above all, traveling gives you mental clarity to figure out how to live with intent. It's a way to guide your life, not just wait for things to happen.

Travel Tips & Stuff
What You Need to Know

How to get started:

P lanning your trip should be one of the most exciting things about it. You want to be spontaneous, but it is also very wise to plan your route, so you can take full advantage of all the time and miles you will invest.

- First, decide your passions. If you love airplanes, trains, or old vehicles, plan your trip around that. If you love gardens or architecture, seek that out as the focus of your trip.

- Next, read and research areas of the country that will let you enjoy what you are interested in.

- Make a list by state and city or town, of what you want to see.

- Take your handy road atlas and locate the areas on the pages.

- Make a tentative route plan, so you have an idea of where you are going.

Travel tip: Avoid trying to plan your trip down to a schedule of days, hours, or minutes. On a road trip, it will be virtually impossible to know where you will be on any given day. If you adhere to a schedule, you are more likely to stress out, and less likely to actually enjoy yourself, which is the whole point.

What you need:

You need to bring along a sense of adventure and a curious mind. You need to ditch the idea of always being on a schedule, and live a little more spontaneously to thoroughly enjoy yourself. Things will happen as you travel, both good things and bad things, and you need to prepare your mind and your soul for day-to-day changes.

So much of our lives are planned out. Between growing up, going to school, finding a career, marriage, kids, or whatever, people have lost much of the ability to be spontaneous. But you must take spontaneity on the trip with you, because you may make detours along the way to see something really spectacular.

So, for the practical stuff you need:

A great vehicle-I am now five years into the trip and have swapped out my Honda CRV for a small RV, just under 20 feet. I go small because I see humongous RVs on the road, towing a car behind, and all I can think of is, they can't go just anywhere. They are too big. Bad gas mileage, cumbersome to drive, slow, and not agile like my small RV. So, I encourage you, if you want to go car or RV camping and be able to go on remote dirt roads, get an agile vehicle, and small RVs are great.

Travel tip: Don't be afraid to do some modifications to your vehicle. I have made many alterations to my RV, including changing the plumbing, which used to be a mere 4 inches off of the ground, so I would break it all the time. It's now encased in my outside storage compartment. I am also a minimalist, so I have jettisoned anything I won't use or don't love. Don't be afraid to get rid of unnecessary stuff.

An awesome camera that you know inside and out. I use a Nikon and it takes wonderful pictures. Don't skimp on a camera, and don't think a cellphone camera is all you need, because you want the best for your beautiful photos.

Window shades-the best ones are magnetic so you just place them against your windows and they cling to them, obscuring the view inside your car. I also have magnetic window screens, so I can leave my windows down with no bugs!

Battery operated fans and lights-these are important, so you don't have to rely on your house batteries for light and cooling options.

Portable air compressor-this little gem plugs into your cigarette lighter and will inflate your tires if you have a flat. Make sure the air compressor can reach to all of your tires, including your rear tires.

Portable battery charger and power bank-mine comes with battery cables and the power bank, yet once inside the case, it is small enough to put in your glove compartment. This little item, unfortunately, I have had to use, and it saved me.

Portable generator-I have two gas powered generators on the back of my RV, which are hooked together with a coupling unit. I have an interior generator, but after much expense and multiple repairs, it still doesn't work. Now I have generators which will run everything, including AC, and I can maintain them myself.

All season clothing-you never know what different states will bring for weather, so take hot weather and cold weather clothes, and a fair amount of shoes appropriate for hiking, or walking, sandals, and slippers, which are nice at night. Also take along a pair of cheap rubber flip-flops to wear in the public showers you might go into.

Your own pillows-I like my own pillows, so I don't wake up with neck cramps, especially after sleeping in the car.

Sleeping bag and cozy blankets-you want to stay warm and layering is everything.

Warm hat, warm socks, and fuzzy jammies to keep you warm for cold nights sleeping in the car.

A great road atlas, and great guidebooks-get one that's easy to read, with great pictures. For a road atlas, just get one that is easy to read.

A word about photography:

Along with a great camera, you need to have a great eye. This is easier than it sounds once you have worked with your camera and are comfortable taking pictures with it. I am not a professional photographer, but I like my pictures and other people do too.

These are my tips for taking great pictures:

- Experiment with taking both horizontal and vertical shots.

- Don't always put the subject of the photo in the middle of the photograph.

- This one is important: pay attention to the foreground, and if possible, have something, a plant or whatever, in the foreground to help give the photo dimension and depth.

- This one is important too: turn around often to see the view you just came from. I do this quite often and some of my best pictures have resulted from when I turned around and took the shot.

You can also take a mental photo. Place an image in your mind that you can call upon later. Use all of your senses to see, hear, smell, and maybe even to taste, what is around you. You have the means to fully experience your surroundings, and that is very important to a traveler. When you take a mental photo, be sure to jot down quick little details about what you saw, heard, smelled, or tasted, so you can jog your memory later.

And last, but not least...don't be posing in front of everything, everywhere, to show that you actually went somewhere. Most people want to see themselves in your photo and be mentally transported there, but they can't if you are there already.

To camp or not to camp:

Car or RV camping is great. I prefer it to sleeping on the cold, hard ground in a tent. I can lock the doors, put my window shades up and be cozy for the night.

Some people camp in a Walmart parking lot and feel safe. I do not. I believe that if you are in a busy area, you are more likely to be confronted by a nut job who may bother you. Nothing against Walmart, and many Walmart stores don't allow overnight parking. I don't go for rest areas either because they have a track record of incidents happening to people in rest areas, especially women travelers.

I have come to love casino parking lots. I enjoy gambling, so for a little money, many casinos will provide overnight stays if you gamble a little inside the casino. I also do a lot of boondocking, because it's free, and I believe you are safer parked out in the middle of nowhere in the dark.

I also enjoy camping In state or national campgrounds, wildlife sanctuaries, and fairgrounds.

A word about safety:

When you are a woman traveling alone, it's critical to keep a low profile. Don't tell people you are traveling alone, where you are staying, or any other personal information.

I don't go to bars or get drunk. I'm not preaching but you are on your own, in a city or town you've never been to, and you don't know anyone, so it's not the time to lose control of what you are doing. When you are in control, you are better able to decide which people you want to get to know better.

Travel tip: If you feel vulnerable traveling alone, that's OK. Vulnerability is part of passion, and traveling is a passionate thing to do. You can put one of those family stickers on your vehicle to indicate to others that you are not traveling alone, which can help you feel more secure.

Maintain your connections:

When you are traveling alone, there is a definite sense of disconnection. It feels almost like you are the only one in the world, traveling through space and time. That's why it's critical to keep your connections to loved ones active.

Be on Facebook while you are traveling. You may not have internet a lot of the time, or the internet will be poor. Consider paying to have your phone be a hotspot. It's a little bit of money per month, but it's worth it and has saved me from being without internet. I love the convenience of it, and you will too.

Plan your journey around visiting family members or friends you haven't seen for a long time, or people that are good friends. When you see people you know, it will ground you, so you can continue traveling.

Check in by phone with loved ones. They worry about you, and it's good for both of you to stay connected no matter where you are.

Consider traveling with a pet. I now travel with my 12 year-old sheltie Rosie, after losing my beloved sheltie, Sadie. Rosie is a wonderful companion. She is also an excellent watchdog, and barks her head off at other dogs and people.

Travel tip: One of the easiest and best ways I stay connected while traveling is to offer to take a photo for someone I don't know. Many couples, families, or singles would love to have more pictures of themselves traveling. It's an easy and quick way to have a connection with a fellow traveler, and it's good manners too.

Practical matters:

You need to have an address to send your mail to. Keep in touch with whomever is nice enough to do this for you.

You will also need to come back occasionally to register your car, vote, go to doctor visits, and take care of any other business. You can't leave it all behind, as tempting as that may be.

Bad things that happened:

I have had a few problems, mostly associated with my RV. I bought an older model, vintage 1999, and I have had to do a few repairs.

My worst experience came when I took my rig in to a shop in Spokane, Washington (who shall remain nameless.) All I needed was an oil change. I got the oil change and was about an hour south of town on a Friday at 4:30, when my engine blew.

I was in the middle of the eastern Washington prairie, many miles from the nearest town. All I could do was watch my oil drain out onto the Interstate. I can't help but think it was associated with my oil change, but I couldn't prove it. The moral of this story is: DON'T LET JUST ANYONE WORK ON YOUR VEHICLE.

Good things that happened:

I have met many great people on my travels, from all walks of life. I have also learned not to judge people. I have met numerous homeless people who are often just wanting a kind word, and not to be treated like dirt.

People have mistaken me for a homeless person, and I too, have been treated like dirt. When I can, I try to help people and be kind to them. Most of the time, they smile and reciprocate. You will always meet people who are unkind, but they are just as likely to be driving a huge expensive rig, or to be homeless.

We are all Americans, and we are all part of the human race. When you meet people across the country, you realize just how important it is to get to know your fellow citizens, and learn more about how they view the world and our country.

I have to give a special shout-out to the many dedicated people, often volunteers, who staff our state and national parks and monuments. They work tirelessly to ensure the health of our natural resources, and help travelers enjoy their visit. The same is true of the many people who staff the museums in small towns and large cities. They enjoy history, like I do, and it shows in their smiles.

Along with wonderful people, I have seen an America that is spectacularly beautiful, with open prairies, majestic mountains, and crystal clear rivers. I have seen a small fraction of the history of our country. I have seen the memorials to the brave people who shaped our country. I have fallen in love with America in a way that was not possible sitting in my living room. People ask me, "would I do it again?" The answer comes easily, "Yes, in a heartbeat."

Index
Referenced by Sections

C

Bibliography &
Further Reading

California Trail, National Park Service

Donovan, James, *A Terrible Glory*, Back Bay Books, New York, NY, 2008

Enss, Chris, *Tales Behind theTombstones*, Twodot Publishing, 2007

Finch, etc. al.., Jackie. *Eyewitness Travel USA*. DK Publishing, 2017

Fort Sisseton Historic State Park Walking Tour Guide, 2019

Glassman, Steve, *It Happened on the Santa Fe Trail*, Morris Book Publishing, Guilford, CT, 2008

Griffith, T.D., *Deadwood: The Best Writings on the Most Notorious Town in the West*, TwoDot Press, Helena, Mt. 2010

Historic Keystone Walking Tour, Keystone Area Historical Society

Jones, Landon Y. *The Essential Lewis and Clark*. HarperCollins Publishers, 2000

Laskin, David, *The Children's Blizzard*, Harper Collins, New York, NY, 2004

Lewis, Chad and Fisk, Terry, *The South Dakota Road Guide To Haunted Locations*, Unexplained Research Publishing Company, 2006

Parker, Watson and Lambert, Hugh K. Lambert, *Black Hills Ghost Towns*, The Swallow Press, Chicago, IL, 1974

The Mammoth Site: A Self-guided Tour

Mayo, Matthew, *Haunted Old West*, Rowman & Littlefield, Guilford, CT, 2012

Mormon Trail, National Park Service

National Parks of the Midwest, National Park Service

Oregon Trail, National Park Service

Rutter, Michael. *Bedside Book of Bad Girls: Outlaw Women of the American West*, Farcountry Press, 2008.

Shadley, Mark, and Wennes, Josh, *Haunted Deadwood*, The History Press, 2012

Wagner, Tricia Martineau, *It Happened on the Oregon Trail*, Morris Book Publishing, 2014

About the Author

Julie Bettendorf is a world traveler with a degree in archaeology and a background in history. She has traveled extensively throughout Egypt, Central America, South America, Europe, and the United Kingdom, visiting archaeological and historical sites all along the way.

Currently, Julie is traveling around the US visiting ghost towns, ancient rock art sites, and archaeological wonders as part of research for her ongoing historical travel series entitled ***Wandering Woman***. Wandering Woman is a set of state-by-state guides, full of photographs, historical anecdotes, and unique tips to help other women travel and explore solo across the US by car. Julie enjoys writing freelance blogs, traveling frequently with her two adult children, and hiking outdoors with her faithful dog companion Rosie.

Also By Julie Bettendorf

    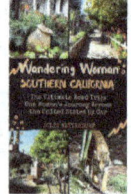

Wandering Woman: South Dakota is the fifteenth book in the ***Wandering Woman Travel Series***. Additional books are available, including ***Kansas, Nebraska, Montana***, ***Colorado, Utah, Nevada, Arizona, Oregon, Washington, Idaho, New Mexico, Wyoming, Northern California,*** and ***Southern California*** in ebook and paperback.

Julie has published two children's books in an ongoing, beautifully illustrated travel series entitled ***Anthony Ant Goes to France*** and ***Anthony Ant Goes to Egypt***.

She has also published a work of historical fiction entitled ***Luxor: Book of Past Lives*** which has recently been released as an audiobook, read by renowned narrator Barry Shannon.